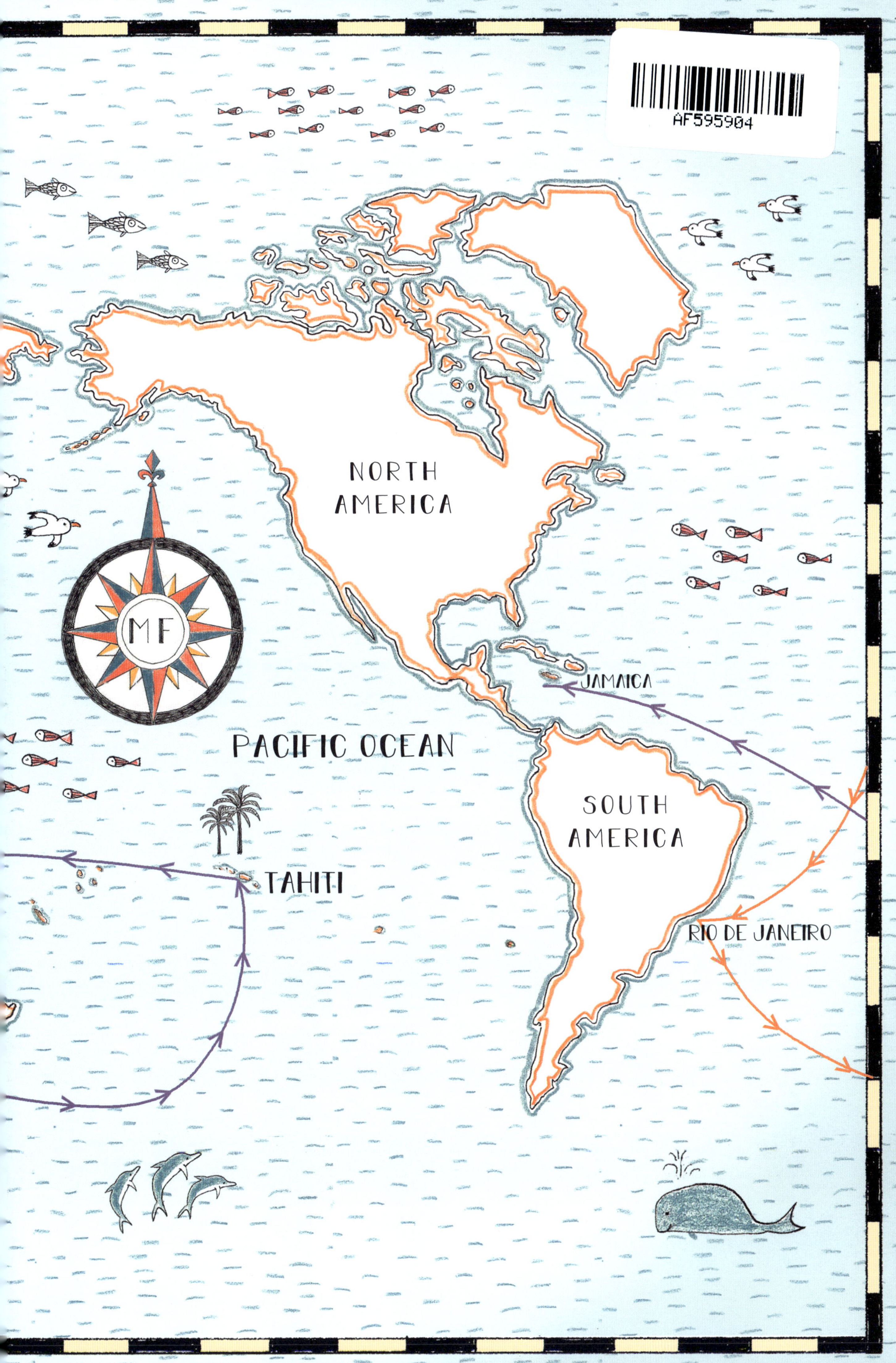
NORTH
AMERICA
MF
PACIFIC OCEAN
JAMAICA
SOUTH
AMERICA
TAHITI
RIO DE JANEIRO

First published in 2020 by
wild dog
Abbotsford Convent
1 St Heliers Street
Abbotsford Vic 3067
Australia
wdog.com.au

Reprinted 2021 (twice)

Printed and bound in China by
Everbest Printing Co. Ltd.

ISBN: 9781742034935 (hbk)

Wild Dog would like to thank Neil Conning for his careful fact checking and thorough proofreading.

The illustrations in this book were created with ink and coloured pencil.

10 9 8 7 6 5 4 3 22 23 24

A catalogue record for this book is available from the National Library of Australia

FSC® is a non-profit international organisation established to promote the responsible management of the world's forests.

For Banjo, who loves to explore (and also likes cats).

C.W.

To Jacko and Felix,
may you sail through life with fresh breezes and fine weather.

P.P.

CAROLE WILKINSON is an internationally award-winning and best-selling author.

Her *Dragonkeeper* series has sold all over the world and is currently being made into a film.

Carole's non-fiction title, *Ten Pound Pom*, won the 2018 Primary Educational Picture Book of the Year and was shortlisted for the 2018 CBCA Picture Book of the Year.

Her most recent picture books are *Putting Australia on the Map*, and *Earth Matters – Loving Our Planet*, illustrated by Hilary Cresp, also published by Wild Dog Books.

Carole lives in Melbourne.

PRUE PITTOCK is an illustrator and artist living by the sea on the beautiful Mornington Peninsula, in Victoria.

Prue's bush studio is full of pencils, ink, paint, and lots of light — all this and a keen imagination and passion to turn a great story into a great picture book.

Matthew Flinders — Adventures on Leaky Ships is her fifth illustrated book.

MATTHEW FLINDERS

ADVENTURES ON LEAKY SHIPS

CAROLE WILKINSON

ILLUSTRATED BY

PRUE PITTOCK

MATTHEW FLINDERS joined the British Royal Navy when he was sixteen. It was a shock to his father. His mother died when he was only nine. He was expected to become a doctor like his father and grandfather.

It wasn't Matthew's childhood in the quiet English village of Donington that made him long for adventures at sea, it was a book called *Robinson Crusoe*.

Matthew first sailed to Tahiti under Captain Bligh (famous for surviving the mutiny on the *Bounty*). He was then posted on a warship that took part in a battle with the French. The ship lost two masts, the captain lost a leg, but this experience didn't give Matthew a taste for war. His dream was to sail to unknown lands like his hero Captain Cook. Fortunately, exploration was part of the Royal Navy's work.

Matthew next served on the *Reliance*, a leaky old ship that was sailing to Britain's most distant colony, New South Wales. His brother Samuel, aged thirteen, was also on board.

On the seven-month voyage, Matthew became friends with ship's surgeon George Bass. They wanted to continue exploring the New South Wales coast that Captain Cook himself had left unfinished.

When the *Reliance* docked at Port Jackson in 1795, the town of Sydney was just seven years old. The 3400 inhabitants, mainly

convicts, were struggling to grow crops in a strange land. They relied on food shipped from England to survive. Many things were in short supply — including ships. No one was about to offer two young men a vessel for exploration. Luckily, George Bass had come prepared. As well as his medicines and doctor's equipment, he'd brought with him a small boat, less than 2.5 metres long, called *Tom Thumb*.

Six weeks after their arrival in Port Jackson, Matthew and George set sail. They had two *Tom Thumb* adventures along the southern coast of New South Wales, surviving storms and uncomfortable nights at sea. Aboriginal men showed them where to find water. Matthew's way to thank them was to offer to cut their hair. They accepted!

Naval duties called them back to the *Reliance* and they sailed to the Cape of Good Hope to buy cattle and sheep for the colony. In Cape Town, Matthew took naval exams and became Second Lieutenant Flinders.

On the return voyage, a litter of kittens was born on board the ship. Matthew adopted one and called him Trim. A fearless kitten, he was soon climbing the masts ... and falling overboard. Matthew rescued him and Trim became his special companion.

While Matthew had duties on the *Reliance*, George Bass had another adventure. He sailed a whaleboat around the coast and discovered a large bay (in present-day Victoria), which he named Western Port.

When he had free time again, Matthew volunteered as a crew member on the *Francis*. This ship sailed to the Furneaux Islands off the north-eastern tip of Van Diemen's Land (Tasmania) to salvage cargo and rescue men from a shipwreck. Matthew drew a sea chart of the area. He named one group of tiny islands the Chappell Isles. This was a clue to where his thoughts were wandering while he worked.

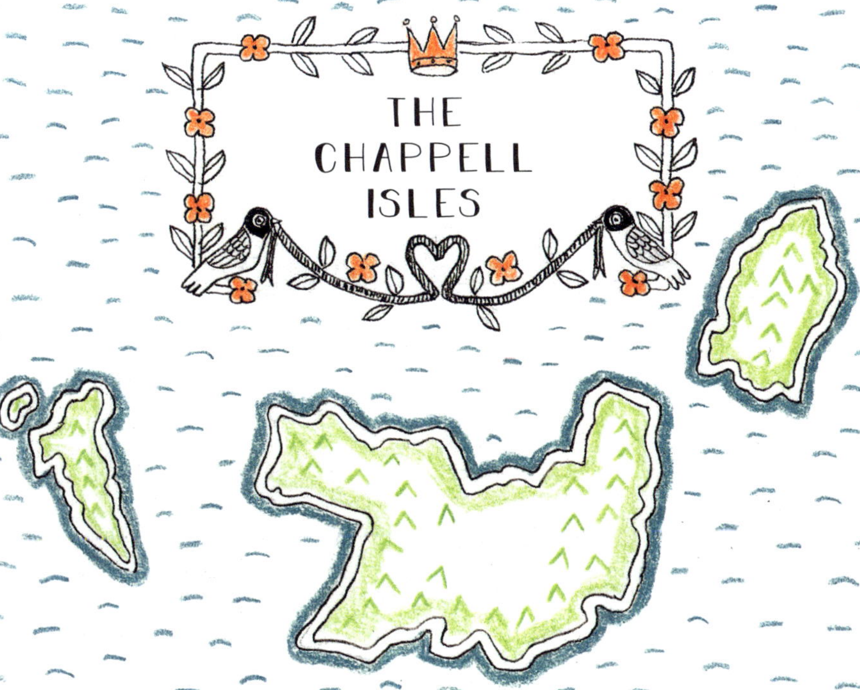

Back in Port Jackson, Matthew and George compared notes. They'd been sailing on opposite sides of a narrow stretch of water. Earlier sailors had decided that Van Diemen's Land was joined to New South Wales, but Matthew and George were sure they'd been sailing in a strait. Governor Hunter allowed them to use the 25-tonne *Norfolk* to prove their theory. She leaked, but Matthew and George didn't care.

They set sail, Matthew in command, a crew of eight and George Bass to record the plants and animals they saw. They also took a man named Bungaree to help communicate with Aboriginal people they met. Trim went too.

High seas threatened to sink the *Norfolk*. Ferocious gales drove her backwards. Eight weeks passed, and they were still struggling to make headway along the top of Van Diemen's Land.

When the coast started to curve north, it looked as if Van Diemen's Land was joined to the mainland after all. But the next day, the *Norfolk* sailed into the Indian Ocean. It was 28 years since Cook had landed in Botany Bay, 10 years since the First Fleet arrived. At last Matthew and George had proved Van Diemen's Land was an island.

The discovery of the strait was important as it shortened voyages from England to Port Jackson by at least a week. Matthew suggested it be called Bass's Strait in honour of his friend.

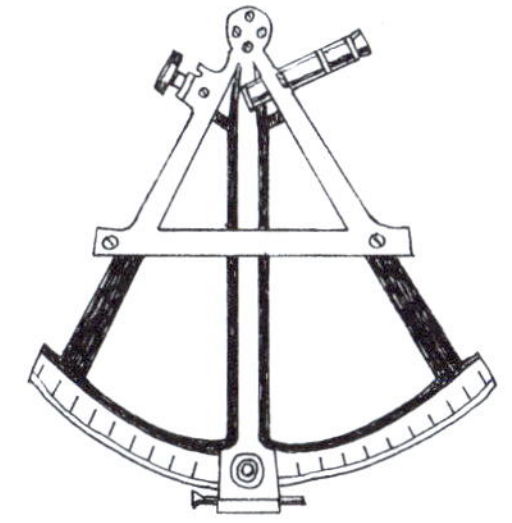

NAVIGATION EQUIPMENT

Sailors have to know their precise position at sea. Latitude is the position north or south of the equator. Longitude is the position east or west, usually measured as the distance from Greenwich in England. Flinders used the stars and the exact time of day to calculate the longitude.

He needed:

a *sextant* to measure the angle between the horizon and the stars, planets, sun or moon when at sea;

a *theodolite* for measuring horizontal and vertical angles on land;

an *azimuth compass* to locate a particular star or other object in the sky; and

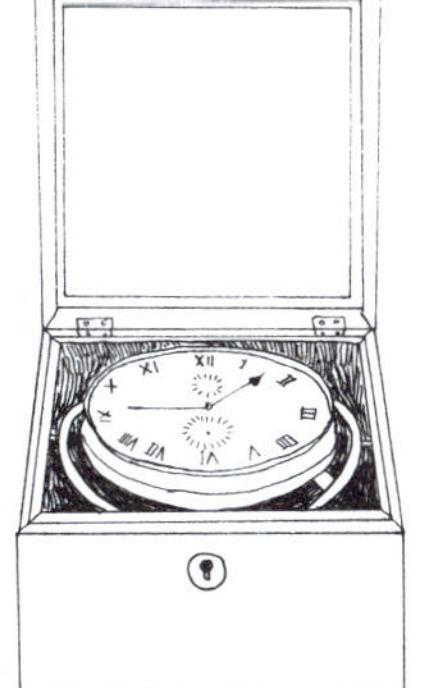

a *marine chronometer*, which was a clock that lost no more than a fraction of a second per day, even on a rocking ship. Sailors have been able to measure latitude for centuries. Accurate measurement of longitude wasn't possible until 1761 when Englishman John Harrison invented the first marine chronometer. They were still unreliable when Flinders was sailing, so he had six chronometers on board.

George Bass had enjoyed these adventures, but he hated navy life. He left the navy and went in search of his fortune, trading goods around the world. Matthew's best friend disappeared from his life.

It was time for the *Reliance* to return to England. On the long voyage home, Matthew thought about his own future. His passion for exploration and discovery hadn't diminished. He didn't need a fortune. He wanted to complete the map of *Terra Australis*, leaving nothing for other explorers to discover.

As soon as he arrived in England, Matthew wrote to Sir Joseph Banks, the botanist on Captain Cook's first voyage. Matthew asked him to convince the Admiralty that another voyage of exploration to *Terra Australis* was necessary.

A new voyage wasn't Matthew's only wish. He also wrote to Ann Chappell, a young lady who was a friend of his sisters. He told her that off the coast of distant Van Diemen's Land, there was a group of islands that he'd named after her. What more proof of his love did she need?

Sir Joseph agreed that a new voyage of discovery to *Terra Australis* was essential — and urgent. The French were planning a similar expedition. They could be planning to stake a claim on the continent.

With England at war with France, the only ship available was a coal carrier that needed repairing before it was fit for exploration. Matthew hardly noticed her shortcomings. He thought she was exactly the sort of ship that Captain Cook would have chosen. She was renamed the *Investigator*.

Matthew visited Ann. Her father had been a sailor. She did not want the lonely life of a sailor's wife. Matthew was heartbroken, but the French expedition had already left.

Matthew was in a hurry to set sail. He received his commission to command the *Investigator*. Captain Flinders was in charge of 82 men— the officers and crew including his brother Samuel as second lieutenant and the men Matthew called his scientific gentlemen:

an astronomer to assist with navigation,
a botanist to study plants,
two artists to paint pictures of what they saw,
and a gardener to look after living plant specimens.

There were also 12 marines for protection.

Top row left to right: astronomer John Crosley, botanist Robert Brown, landscape artist William Westall, botanical artist Ferdinand Bauer.

Bottom row: Second Lieutenant Samuel Flinders, a marine, a ship's boy, gardener Peter Good.

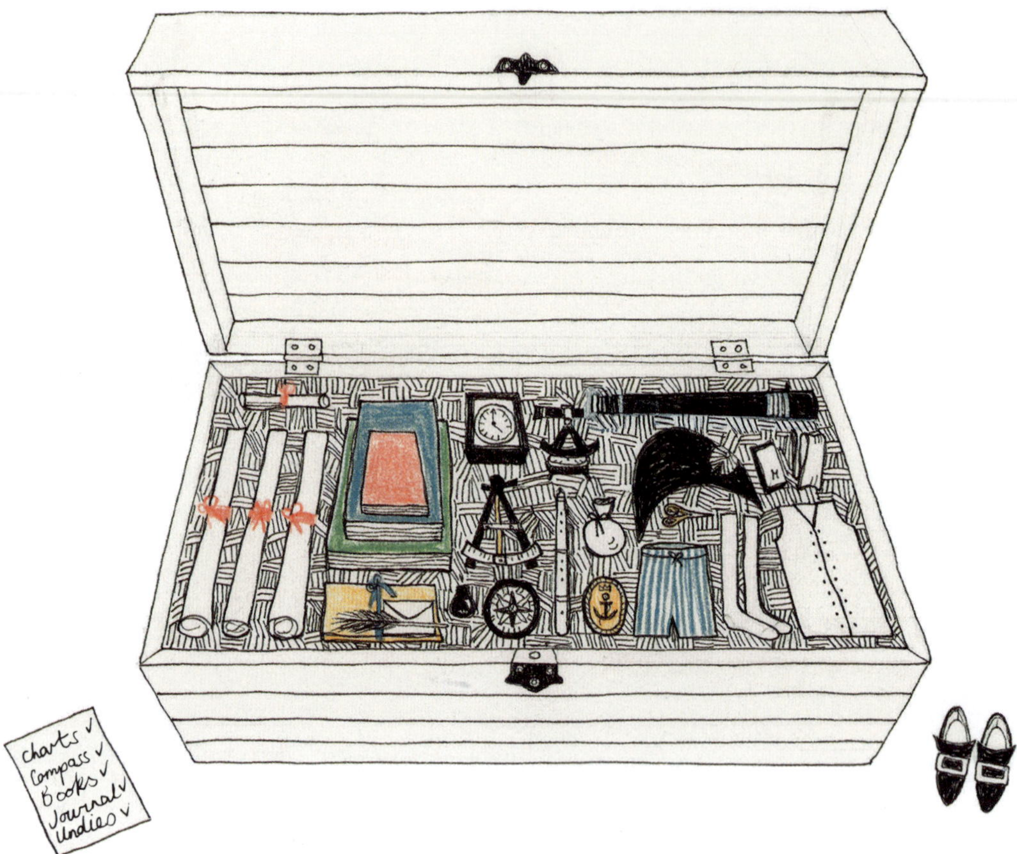

To help him guide his ship across the world, Matthew took charts of the southern seas, the journals of other explorers, and 15 volumes of the *Encyclopaedia Britannica*, borrowed from Sir Joseph.

The *Investigator* needed a passport allowing her to stop at French ports, even when England and France were at war. While he waited for it to arrive, Matthew had time to think. He couldn't bear the thought of leaving Ann behind. He told her she could sail with him on the voyage. Ann relented. They were married in secret.

They needed to set sail before the Admiralty found out Ann was on board. But luck wasn't on their side. An officer came to inspect the ship. He found Mrs Flinders in Matthew's cabin.

Sir Joseph told Matthew he must choose between his wife or the voyage. Ann knew what his choice would be. In a hidden place in Matthew's cabin she painted some flowers. In tiny letters, she wrote 'Forget me not'.

The passport arrived from France. After three months of marriage, Matthew set sail, leaving Ann behind. Trim went with him.

As soon as they left the English Channel, the *Investigator* started to leak. When they reached the Cape of Good Hope, she already needed recaulking. Matthew was disappointed that there were no letters from Ann waiting for him.

To keep his crew healthy, Matthew ordered them to regularly scrub the decks and sprinkle them with vinegar. He bought fresh meat, fruit and vegetables at ports. The men were given lime juice or sauerkraut every day to prevent them from getting scurvy. To keep them happy, music and dancing were allowed in the evenings.

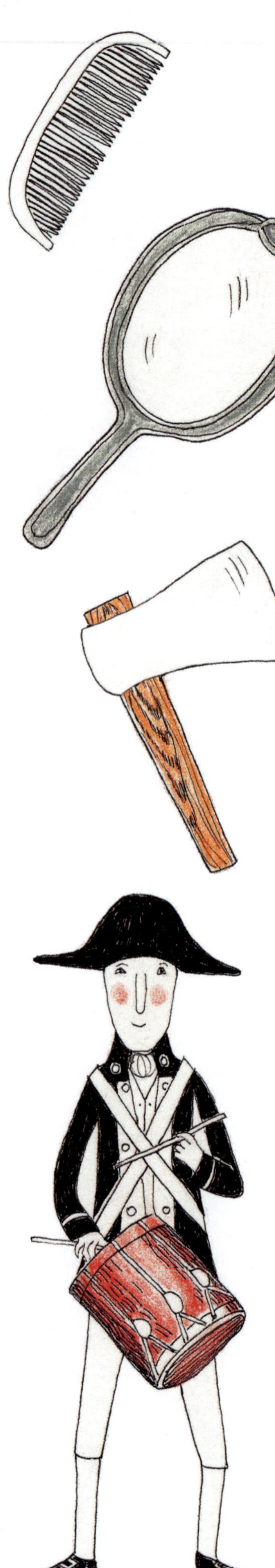

As they sailed across the Indian Ocean, there was good weather. The pumps coped with the small amount of leakage. After five months at sea, they reached Cape Leeuwin, the south-west tip of *Terra Australis*.

They headed east along what was called the Unknown Southern Coast, even though three other European ships had already sailed that way. Following a 150-year-old Dutch map, Matthew began making his own detailed chart of that coast.

While ashore searching for fresh water, they met some Aboriginal men who were friendly and inquisitive about the strangers. The navy had provided Matthew with gifts for Aboriginal people he met — mirrors, beads, combs, simple tools. The Nyungar weren't interested in the trinkets, but they all wanted one of the tomahawks. To impress the Aboriginal men, Matthew brought ashore his marines and marched them along the beach. The Nyungar men were very interested in the soldiers' red coats crossed with white belts, and the music made by fife and drum.

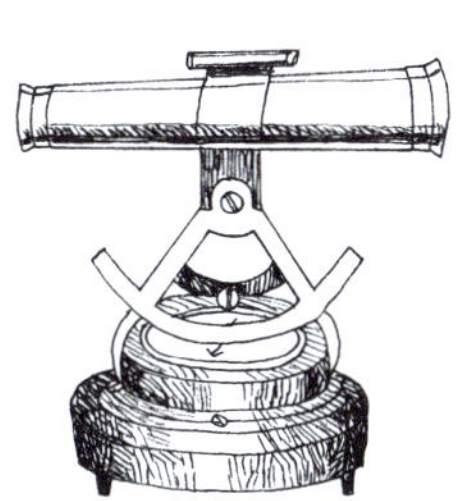

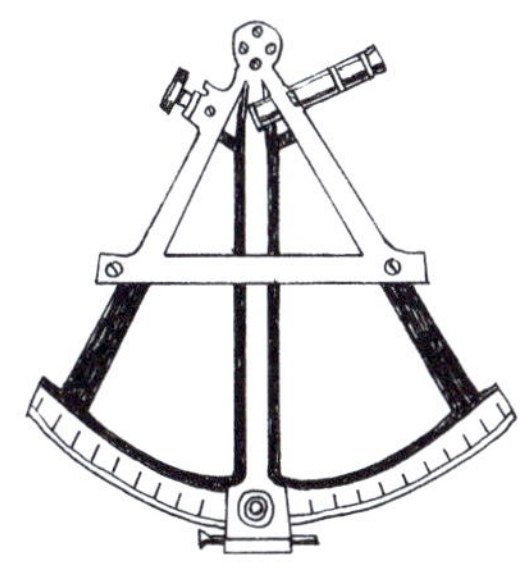

Matthew sailed the *Investigator* as close to shore as possible without risk of running aground or crashing into rocks. He took measurements using his navigation equipment. He often went ashore to take bearings. John Thistle, the ship's master, accompanied him. Mr Thistle was a reliable man who had been Matthew's shipmate since the *Reliance*. Every evening, Matthew made a rough chart of the coastline. With future sailors in mind, he recorded dangerous reefs and sandbanks, as well as safe harbours and places where fresh water could be found.

Halfway round the Great Australian Bight, the Dutch chart came to a sudden end. Matthew would be the first to survey the rest of the southern coast. There was a theory that *Terra Australis* couldn't possibly be one big island, that it must be divided by a strait. Matthew wanted to be the one to discover it. There was great excitement when a gap in the coastline more than 6 kilometres wide came into view. They couldn't see an end to it. Surely this was the strait that would lead all the way through to the Gulf of Carpentaria!

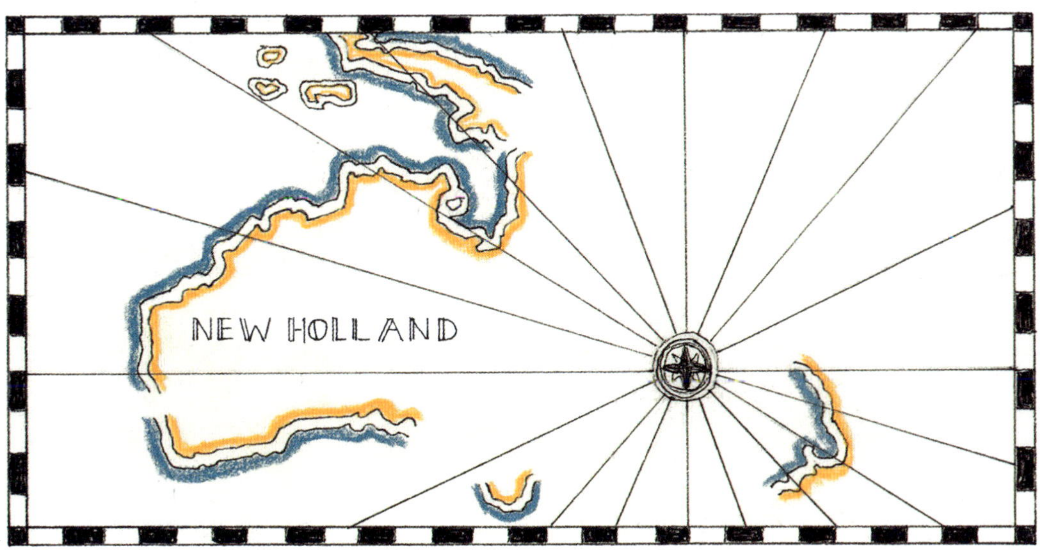

Mr Thistle went ashore to search for much needed fresh water. He never returned. A search party found his wrecked boat, but not the ship's master or his crew. That evening, one of the sailors told the tale of Mr Thistle visiting a fortune teller just before they set sail. The man had told him he was about to go on a long sea voyage. And he would drown.

Matthew was devastated. To add to his misery, there was no strait, just an enormous gulf. He named it Spencer's Gulf.

They spent time on Kangaroo Island studying the teeming wildlife. Matthew also shot kangaroos for food. Their stores were dwindling, and he had 74 men to feed.

Soon after, they sailed into a sheltered bay, a sailor on lookout duty called out that there was a white rock ahead. As they drew closer, they realised it was actually a sail.

Matthew was astonished. This was the first ship they had encountered since the Cape of Good Hope. It was *le Géographe* — one of the French ships commanded by Captain Nicolas Baudin! Matthew rowed across to meet his rival. Baudin had lost his nine-month lead. His crew was mutinous. More than 50 men had left the ship. Baudin had just sailed around Van Diemen's Land, but didn't realise that Matthew had drawn up the chart he'd been following!

Matthew named the meeting place Encounter Bay. He continued east, pleased he'd beaten Baudin to the Unknown Southern Coast.

A month later, the *Investigator* dropped anchor in Port Jackson. Matthew had sailed his ship halfway around the world, making accurate charts as he went. His crew was healthier than when they'd left England — and just as happy.

Matthew reported to the new Governor of New South Wales, Philip Gidley King, who offered him any assistance needed to complete the voyage, including a second ship, the *Lady Nelson*. Matthew was pleased that Bungaree could again join him. While the crew prepared the ships, Matthew worked on his charts.

When *le Géographe* arrived in Port Jackson, Baudin's crew was sick and dying from scurvy and dysentery. Just twelve men were fit to work. Governor King supplied them with everything they needed, including scarce fresh meat. Matthew had to purchase his own — sheep, pigs, geese and chickens. He also bought 13 tonnes of ship's biscuit.

To Matthew's great joy, letters from Ann finally arrived.

The two ships set sail. Matthew's plan was to circumnavigate the entire continent, mapping 35,000 kilometres of coast. First he retraced Captain Cook's journey up the eastern coast, filling in the gaps left by his hero.

On Great Sandy Island, now called Fraser Island, Bungaree was frustrated that the Butchulla people couldn't understand him. He needed them to trust him, so he took off his European clothes so they could see he was like them.

The *Lady Nelson* was slow, her captain too nervous to sail as close to the coast as Matthew did. Sometimes Matthew lost sight of her and had to wait for her to catch up.

The monsoon season was approaching. Matthew decided to cut short his coastal survey and head straight to the Gulf of Carpentaria.

The *Investigator* became trapped in coral reefs. High on the masthead, peering through his telescope, Matthew searched for a way through the coral maze. They were sailing so close to the reef, Matthew and his scientists could climb down and walk across it, admiring the colourful coral and fish.

It took two weeks to find a way out to open sea. Matthew named that impenetrable obstacle the Great Barrier Reef. The *Investigator* was undamaged, but the *Lady Nelson* had struck a reef. She'd proved to be more of a nuisance than a help, so Matthew sent her back to Port Jackson.

As the *Investigator* sailed through Torres Strait, Matthew corrected errors on Cook's chart and found a safer, quicker passage between the dangerous reefs and islands.

The ship was leaking badly and needed urgent repairs. In the shelter of the Gulf of Carpentaria, the ship's carpenters examined her hull. Many of the wooden planks were rotten. The carpenters told Matthew the *Investigator* could only survive for six months in fair weather. It was the worst possible news. He would have to return to Port Jackson immediately. And there was no sign of a strait through the continent.

LEAKY SHIPS

Leaking was a constant problem for sailing ships. Ships were made from planks of wood and the small gaps between them were plugged with caulk (strands of old rope mixed with tar) to stop the boat leaking. Rough seas could knock the caulk out. Then it had to be replaced, a process which was called recaulking. On long voyages the planks often rotted. To expose the hull of the ship for repair, if there was no dry dock nearby, the ship had to be run aground on a beach and tilted sideways. This was called careening.

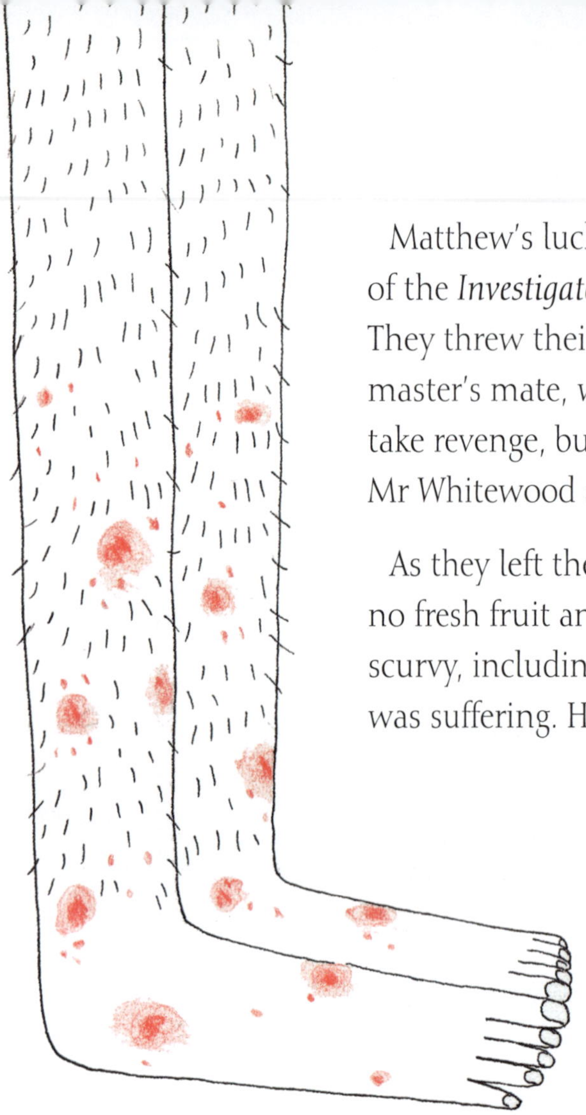

Matthew's luck was running out. While collecting wood, some of the *Investigator*'s crew startled a group of Aboriginal men. They threw their spears at the strangers, and Mr Whitewood, the master's mate, was wounded. Matthew ordered his men not to take revenge, but some ignored him. An Aboriginal man was shot. Mr Whitewood survived.

As they left the gulf, the weather was hot and humid. They had no fresh fruit and vegetables. Twenty-four men had symptoms of scurvy, including Matthew, who had ulcers on his feet. Even Trim was suffering. His claws were falling out.

The ship's surgeon pleaded with Matthew to call into a port to buy fresh food.

Avoiding the monsoons, they sailed west across the top of the continent. It was a longer route, but safer. They stopped at the Dutch settlement on Timor. Matthew bought bananas, oranges, limes and cucumbers for his crew. The local people were unhealthy, and Baudin's crew had got sick there. But Matthew still allowed their water casks to be filled.

Not long after they set sail again, some of the crew became ill with diarrhoea. The bad water from Timor was to blame. Men started to die. Dysentery was sweeping the ship.

When they arrived back in Port Jackson, the *Investigator* was beyond repair and Matthew and his crew were sick.

But as soon as his health improved, Matthew was ready to continue his work. All he needed was a seaworthy ship. None of the ships in Port Jackson were fit for the voyage, and it would take a year for another ship to be sent from England.

The *Porpoise* was about to leave for England, so Matthew decided to join her as a passenger, present his charts to the Admiralty himself and request the best ship they had.

Some of the *Investigator*'s crew stayed in Port Jackson. Some were taken on as crew for the *Porpoise,* while others boarded as passengers. The ship's captain set course well away from the treacherous Great Barrier Reef. Two other ships, the *Bridgewater* and the *Cato*, sailed with the *Porpoise* so they could follow Matthew's safer passage through Torres Strait.

Seven days out from Port Jackson, the *Porpoise* hit a reef and keeled over. One of her masts broke off. The *Bridgewater* and the *Cato* were both trying to avoid the reef. If they were wrecked too, there would be no one to rescue them. In fading light, the *Cato* swerved to avoid colliding with the *Bridgewater* and crashed into the reef. Waves swamped her decks. Her masts disappeared beneath the sea.

The wrecked *Porpoise* lay on her side, waves breaking over her keel, but she stayed in one piece throughout the night. At dawn, Matthew surveyed the disaster. The *Bridgewater* was standing at a distance, unharmed. Matthew assumed her commander, Captain Palmer, was waiting for calmer seas before sending boats to rescue them. He saw a sandbank not far away. Two of the *Porpoise*'s cutters were still afloat. Matthew sent one to rescue the men who had clung to the wreck of the *Cato* all night. Three young boys drowned in the rescue attempt. Matthew took the other boat to inspect the sandbank. It was about one-and-a-half kilometres wide. He saw birds' nests in the sand containing eggs, which convinced him the sandbank stayed dry at high tide.

The sailors salvaged all the provisions they could from their wrecked ship, including some pigs and sheep. They made tents from sails and broken spars. A mast became a flagpole and the British flag was raised upside down — a signal of distress.

The *Bridgewater* had disappeared. They waited four days, but she didn't return. Captain Palmer had abandoned them.

Ninety-four survivors stood on the bleak sandbank, 500 kilometres from shore, with no hope of rescue. Matthew took control of the panicked men. With strict naval discipline, he soon had the island running as smoothly as one of his ships.

He told the men he would sail the ship's cutter to Port Jackson and bring back a ship to rescue them. The cutter was little more than a large rowing boat with a sail, but there were plenty of volunteers to make the dangerous voyage. They named her *Hope*. Matthew gave orders for the men left behind to build two boats from the wreckage of the *Porpoise*. If he didn't return within two months, they were to use them to sail to Port Jackson.

To prove that he wouldn't abandon them, Matthew left behind his brother, his precious charts — and Trim. He set sail in the *Hope*, with an officer and a crew of 12. Those left behind trusted Captain Flinders completely. They turned their flag the right way up.

The first part of the journey was across open sea. The tiny *Hope* plunged through huge waves day and night. If the wind was favourable, they raised the sails. If not, six men rowed. It took three days to reach the east coast of *Terra Australis*. Then they sailed as close to shore as possible, reaching Port Jackson after an epic journey of 250 nautical leagues (1388 kilometres) in 12 days.

Matthew, windblown and unshaven, burst in on Governor King while he was eating dinner. King ordered three ships to be made ready for a rescue mission. One was about to sail to China and would take survivors to Canton, where they could board a ship to England. Another would bring more survivors back to Port Jackson. After the rescue, Matthew would sail the third ship, the *Cumberland*, straight to England. He hadn't given up his plan.

The *Cumberland* was a fraction of the size of other ships Matthew had sailed across oceans, just 29 tonnes. But he was confident he could sail her halfway around the world. Governor King told him not to stop at the French island of Mauritius.

Meanwhile, the shipwrecked sailors were busy building boats. Only six weeks after *Hope* had left, a sail was spotted on the horizon. Captain Flinders had returned as promised! Matthew stepped ashore to smiling faces and rousing cheers.

The *Cumberland* didn't sail well. In a strong wind, she leaned over so far it was impossible to alter the sails. She was infested with fleas, cockroaches and mice. And, of course, she leaked. Of all the leaky ships Matthew had sailed on, the *Cumberland* was the worst. The pumps could barely cope. But Matthew wasn't turning back. With a crew of just 10 men, he set sail for England.

The *Cumberland*'s pumps kept breaking down. In the middle of the Indian Ocean, only one still worked. Matthew had no choice but to sail to Mauritius for repairs. Soldiers with guns greeted them. Matthew was angry that the island's Governor, Captain-General Decaen, kept him waiting for two hours. Decaen was insulted when Matthew didn't take off his hat. The French passport was useless. It was made out to the *Investigator*, not the *Cumberland*. Decaen accused Matthew of being a spy.

Matthew was a prisoner of the French. Weeks turned to months. He taught himself French and wrote long letters to Ann. Eventually, he was allowed to work on his charts and wander around the island. His crew were freed. His beloved Trim disappeared. It was more than six years before Matthew was released.

After 10 long years, Ann hardly recognised the grey-haired man who returned to her. Matthew spent the next four years finishing his journal and charts.

His job done, he asked his brother Samuel to order a new copy of *Robinson Crusoe* so he could reread it. But Matthew was very unwell. A week later his journal arrived from the printers. He died the next day. He was only 40 years old.

Matthew Flinders devoted his life to exploring the world, fearlessly sailing into the unknown. He created the first complete map of Australia's coastline and an atlas of sea charts, for the knowledge of the world and the safety of sailors. And he gave Australia its name.

FLINDERS' CIRCUMNAVIGATION OF AUSTRALIA

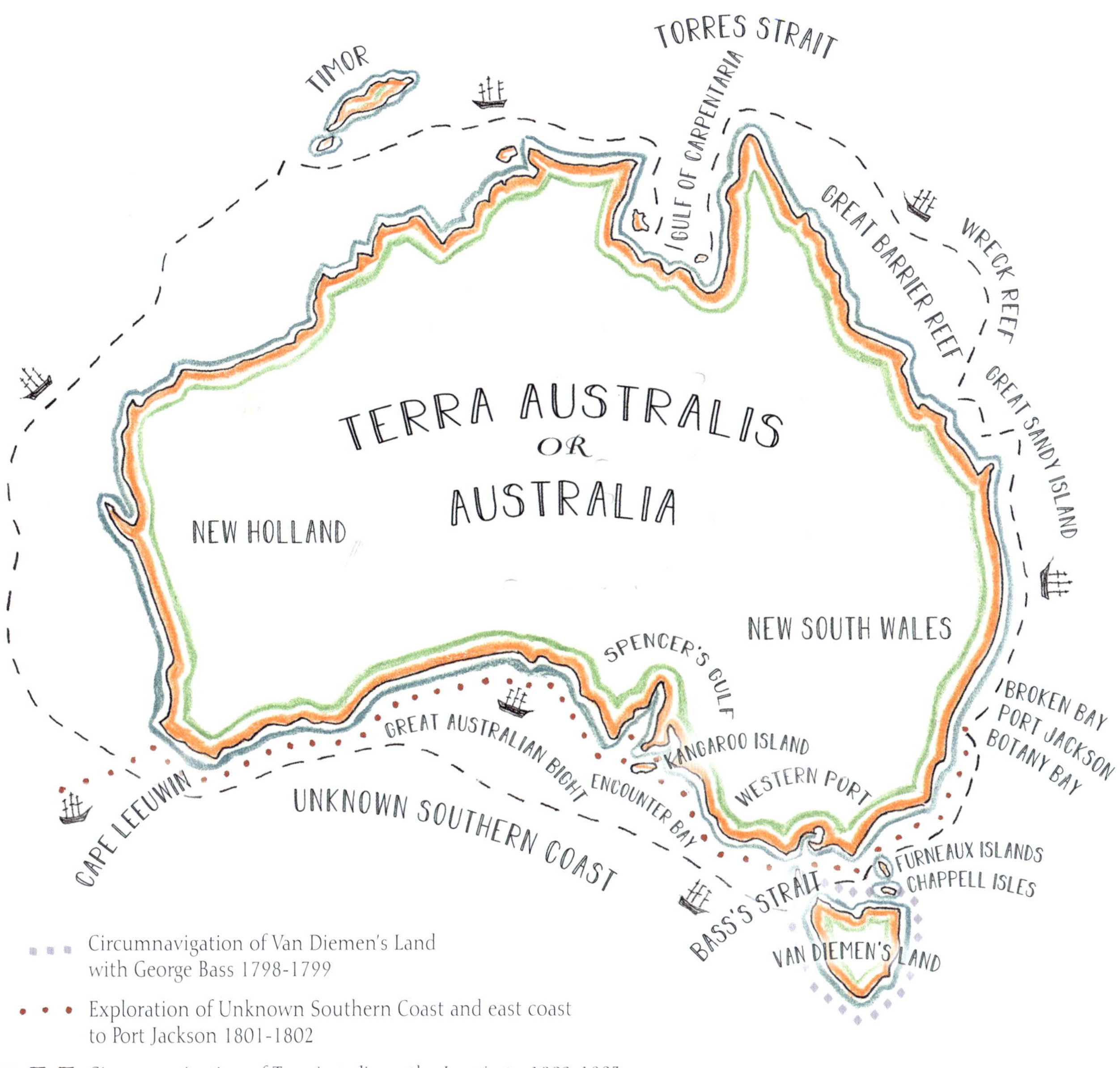

NAMING AUSTRALIA

Dutch explorers had named the western half of the country New Holland in the 1600s, but didn't form a colony here; Captain Cook called the eastern half New South Wales. But after the First Fleet arrived, the country was under British rule, and needed one name. In his journal, Flinders refers to the country as *Terra Australis*, which is Latin for Southern Land. That was what Sir Joseph Banks wanted to call it. Matthew preferred Australia. When he finished his map of the country he called it General Chart of Terra Australis or Australia. Matthew got his way. Australia was a much more popular name, and it became the official name of the country in 1824.

FLINDERS TIMELINE

Birth of Flinders

16 MARCH 1774

Flinders joins the Royal Navy

23 OCTOBER 1789

Voyage to Tahiti on *Providence* with Bligh

4 AUGUST 1791– 7 AUGUST 1793

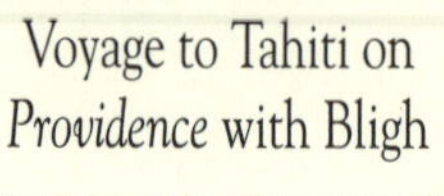

Battle on board *Bellerophon*

1 JUNE 1794

Voyage on *Reliance* to Port Jackson

15 FEBRUARY 1795– 7 SEPTEMBER 1795

Voyage on *Francis* to Furneaux Group

1 FEBRUARY 1798– 9 MARCH 1798

Tom Thumb adventures

26 OCTOBER– 4 NOVEMBER 1795, 25 MARCH – 2 APRIL 1796

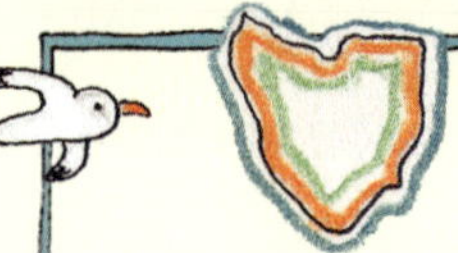

Circumnavigation of Tasmania on the *Norfolk*

7 OCTOBER 1798– 11 JANUARY 1799

Northern coast of NSW on the *Norfolk*

8 JULY–20 AUGUST 1799

Reliance returns to England

3 MARCH 1800– 26 AUGUST 1800

Marriage to Ann Chappell

17 APRIL 1801

Investigator voyage to Port Jackson

18 JULY 1801–9 MAY 1802

Encounter with Baudin

8 APRIL 1802

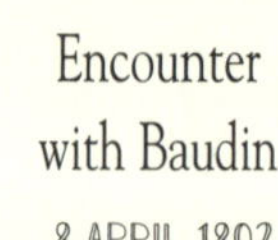

Investigator circumnavigation voyage

22 JULY 1802 – 9 JUNE 1803

Porpoise wrecked

17 AUGUST 1803

Hope sails to Port Jackson

26 AUGUST– 8 SEPTEMBER 1803

Cumberland to Wreck Reef

21 SEPTEMBER 1803

Cumberland voyage to Mauritius

11 OCTOBER– 17 DECEMBER 1803

Imprisonment on Mauritius

17 DECEMBER 1803– 14 JUNE 1810

Return to England

24 OCTOBER 1810

Birth of daughter

1 APRIL 1812

Publication of journal and charts

18 JULY 1814

Death 19 JULY 1814

GLOSSARY

Admiralty, the
The British government department that managed the Royal Navy until 1964.

bearings
The position of a ship at sea measured in degrees of latitude and longitude.

Bungaree
A Kurringgai man born in the Broken Bay area about 1775, who acted as interpreter for Flinders and later Captain Phillip Parker King. He and Flinders became friends. Flinders called him "worthy and brave".

cape
A large piece of land jutting out into the sea.

cutter
A small sailing ship used to carry goods and people between a larger ship and the shore.

dysentry
An infectious disease that causes inflammation of the bowels. It results in bloody diarrhoea. In earlier times it could be fatal.

fife
A small high-pitched flute.

monsoon
A large wind system that changes direction from summer to winter, usually accompanied by heavy rain and strong winds.

mutinous
Not obeying orders.

nautical leagues
A measurement of distance travelled in a ship at sea. One nautical league equals five and a half kilometres.

Port Jackson
The port now called Sydney Harbour.

sauerkraut
Fermented raw cabbage, which is prepared by shredding it and covering it with salt.

scurvy
The first signs of this disease are sores on arms, legs and feet. Then gums start to bleed, wounds won't heal. Someone with untreated scurvy can die from infection or internal bleeding.

In 1753, it was discovered that eating citrus fruit and sauerkraut cured scurvy.1930s scientists learned that scurvy was caused by a lack of Vitamin C. Citrus fruit and sauerkraut both contain Vitamin C.

sea chart
A map for sailors, showing such things as: the depth of the sea around coasts; hazards such as rocks and sandbanks; and information about tides and currents.

ship's biscuit
Hard, tasteless biscuits made with just flour and water that were a large part of a sailor's diet in the 17th and 18th centuries.

spar
A horizontal pole mounted on a ship's mast from which sails are hung.

strait
A narrow passage of water connecting two seas.

survey
To measure the exact dimensions of a piece of land (particularly coasts and islands) in order to draw a sea chart.

Terra Australis
One of the names given to Australia by early explorers.

Van Diemen's Land
Present-day Tasmania.

whaleboat
A long rowing boat that is pointed at both ends so that it can move fast, steered by a long oar.

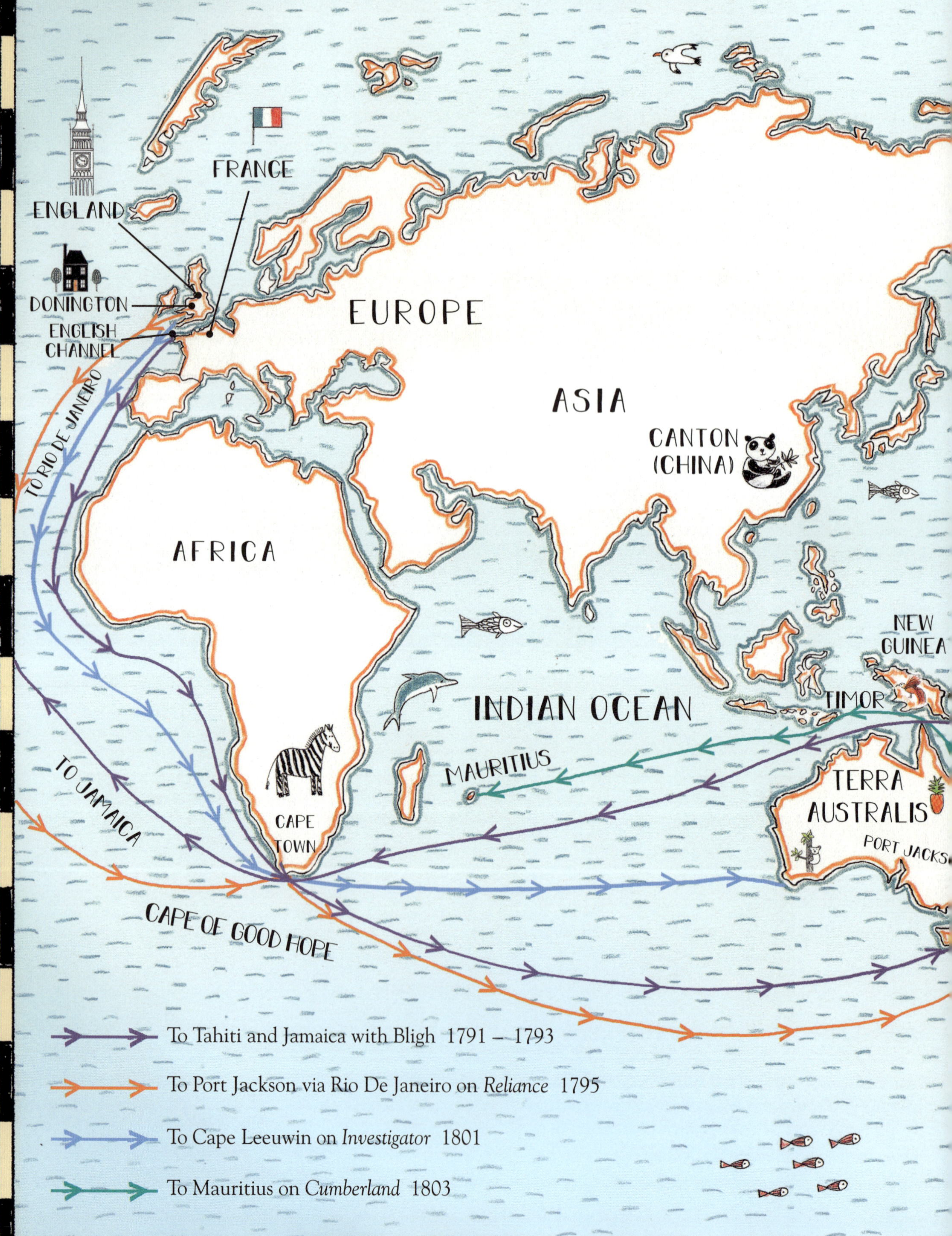
MATTHEW FLINDERS' VOYAGES
ENGLAND
FRANCE
DONINGTON
ENGLISH CHANNEL
EUROPE
ASIA
CANTON (CHINA)
AFRICA
TO RIO DE JANEIRO
INDIAN OCEAN
NEW GUINEA
TIMOR
MAURITIUS
TERRA AUSTRALIS
PORT JACKS
TO JAMAICA
CAPE TOWN
CAPE OF GOOD HOPE
To Tahiti and Jamaica with Bligh 1791 – 1793
To Port Jackson via Rio De Janeiro on *Reliance* 1795
To Cape Leeuwin on *Investigator* 1801
To Mauritius on *Cumberland* 1803